YOUCAT

Confession

GW00383224

YOUCAT

ENGLISH

CONFESSION

Auxiliary Bishop Emeritus Dr. Klaus Dick

Rudolf Gehrig

Bernhard Meuser

Andreas Süß

CATHOLIC TRUTH SOCIETY

Contents

1. GOING TO CONFESSION

2. IN & OUT

THE SACRAMENT OF PENANCE

SPECIAL PRAYERS FOR CONFESSION

Symbols and their meaning:	Quotations from various authors	Quotation from Sacred Scripture
	Information & Tips	YOUCAT questions

3. CONFESSION? – YES, I CAN!

Page 45

Title of the original German edition:
Rudolf Gehrig (Hrsg.): YOUCAT Update! Beichten!
© 2014 YOUCAT Foundation gemeinnützige
GmbH, Königstein im Taunus
Sole shareholder of the YOUCAT Foundation
is the International Pontifical Foundation
Aid to the Church in Need (ACN) in
Königstein in Taunus, Germany.
All rights reserved. The use of the brand is
carried out with the consent of the YOUCAT
Foundation.
YOUCAT® is an internationally registered
and protected brand name and logo. Filed
under GM: 011929131

Design, layout, illustrations: Alexander von
Lengerke, Cologne, Germany

Published by The Incorporated Catholic Truth
Society, 40-46 Harleyford Road,
London, SE11 5AY

© 2018 The Incorporated Catholic Truth Society

ISBN 978-1-78469-555-2

www.youcat.org

Printed and bound in Great Britain
by Bell and Bain Ltd, Glasgow

INSTEAD OF A FOREWORD

When I was 15 years old I had very little experience of the truly liberating effect of confession but a lot has happened since then. I became a priest and now enjoy being able to show young people the beauty of the love and mercy of God in the sacrament of reconciliation – and to experience this again and again myself when I go to confession. I have been privileged to hear countless confessions of young people, and it moves me deeply to see how God frees us from guilt, heals wounds and enables us to experience new life through his forgiveness.

Before the World Youth Day in 2005 I would never have imagined that young people would first be happy to spend six hours together in prayer and singing then go to confession too. This is precisely what happened to a group of young people in Bonn who wanted to relive what they had experienced at the World Youth Day and in various religious communities. This concept is now known as "Nightfever" and is working everywhere. During a Nightfever evening you will see eight to ten priests sitting in the side aisles (sufficiently far apart that no one can hear what is being said). In front of each priest there is a lit candle and a sign indicating what they wish to offer: "Dialogue, blessing, the sacrament of reconciliation". Long queues quickly form behind the signs. Why? Because we receive the liberating power of God's forgiveness in confession and begin again with God, and the joy that is experienced can really be seen. On one occasion a visitor addressed me directly. She had seen how a young woman had left confession completely resolved and happy. It was almost tangible to see the load that had been lifted from her shoulders. So, the woman approached me and said: "That's what I want too." She didn't know exactly how to go to confession but she had seen what happens when you do. That's why I can recommend with all my heart:

Make a new start! Go to confession!

Andreas Süß
Spiritual Director of Nightfever

1.
GOING TO CONFESSION

Why it's great to seek reconciliation with God and how to do it.

Bernhard Meuser

What comes top of the list of things people like doing least? Going to the dentist of course but going to confession comes second.

What? Tell a complete stranger the worst things about myself? Do you think I'm crazy?! Go to a priest and tell him that I have stolen, cheated and lied, or that I wanted the person next to me at school to go to hell or that I'd been surfing awful pages on the Internet? No way! What would he think of me! I wouldn't be able to look him in the eye again!

OK, it's true. You need a lot of courage to be able to face the dark sides of your life.

We all want to be the
Greatest
in some way.

We want to shine. We want to be admired,
and there is a lot that can be admired in us.

+ The one who's a genius at maths
+ The one who's brilliant at sport
+ Or the one who is such a good friend – he would give
  you the shirt off his back if you needed it

But we all know we do
Wrong.

We can try and hide our dark side for a while but one
day it is going to come out that my brilliant homework
is all down to "copy & paste". We soon get caught out
when we've been lying: "So you've been lying to me for
years!" That's when we have to admit that the addiction
had us in its grip. That's when it's painful.

Cowards then look for apologies and make excuses. The brave ones say:

"Yes, I admit it.
I have really
messed
up. Please forgive me!"

In most cases having the courage to confess is rewarded but often we are left with an empty feeling. I once had to speak those difficult words to a friend: "Can you forgive me once again?" What did my friend say? "Ok, I can forgive you but I can't forget!" Hello! What kind of forgiveness is that, I thought, but I quickly replied "then I would prefer you to forget it rather than forgive me!"

Hello God,
I'm still here!

I went to confession again a few days ago. Hello God. I'm still here! I've created rather a mess. I've turned away from you. I know exactly why. Every sin, every lack of kindness affects YOU. You alone are God! Only you can forgive me.

Here I am,
please forgive me!

Even though I have been to confession a few hundred times in my life, I still have to push myself to go, even though I also know that within five minutes of leaving the confessional, I feel as happy as after a swim in the sea.

- + There is peace in my soul.
- + I could sing and dance for joy.
- + Not everyone experiences such a spontaneous joy, but that's how it is for me.

Ok, I wanted to tell you about this special confession. After I had confessed my sins the priest said a few words to me which flowed deep into my soul like balm. "Whenever I absolve you of your sins in the name of Jesus, you really can start again. Just imagine. Completely new! Yes, you begin life again from scratch, and I'll tell you something else:

"God, who is Love, doesn't just *forgive* your sins – he even *forgets* them in a certain sense!"

Wow! I could have given the man a hug!

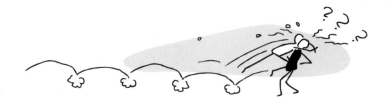

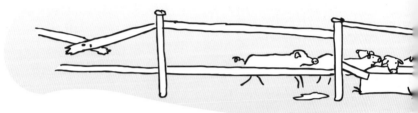

What's God like? Simply unbelievable!

Yes, I often think about this myself. Hey, God, how did I deserve the fact that you're just so interested in me?! You know what I'm like! I really don't have many good things to show for myself.

But clearly that doesn't really interest God. His love is steadfast and what does that make me do? I surrender. I come back like the prodigal son in the Gospel. Sometimes I just can't believe it when our Father in heaven stretches out his arms yet again and welcomes me with joy. I stammer like the prodigal son: "Father, I have sinned against heaven and against you; I am no longer worthy to be called your son!" (*Lk* 15:21).

I just can't believe how God reacts to me, the repentant sinner. Normally you would think, "That's the end of me. His accusing look is going to destroy me! Shouldn't he really say something like 'Stop it! Get out of my sight! I don't want to *ever, ever, ever*

see you again!'" That's exactly what God doesn't do! He is blissfully happy that I have found my way back to him and he has prepared a feast for me. The best of everything!

99 Many people say, "I've done so many bad things that God couldn't possibly forgive me." This is blasphemy. It means you are putting limits on God's mercy which has no limits. His mercy is boundless. Nothing offends our dear Lord more than you doubting his mercy.

JEAN MARIE VIANNEY (CURE D'ARS)

What is Confession?

+ Confession is like performing a **regular**

Update

SPECIAL ☧ UPDATE?

Yes   No

on my life. If I miss the update, then all my software is out-of-date. My laptop is unprotected and exposed to viruses and trojan attacks.

+ Confession is like **taking a car for**

Service.

At least every 30,000 km the car needs to go to the garage. Otherwise it will stop working and the engine will break down. At least once a year – preferably before Easter – every Catholic should go to confession.

+ Confession is like **taking a**

Shower

after a strenuous walk. You come home – dead-tired. The dust from the streets sticks to your skin. You smell and there's no way you can approach others in this state but after a shower you feel like a new person. Your skin can breathe again. You are alive again. You put on fresh clothes.

+ Confession is like the **happy relief after getting**

Back on track.

When you sin, it is like driving in the wrong lane with 160 things on your mind. If you want to avoid a crash, you only have one chance. Turn the car around and drive in the opposite direction!

Perhaps you can think of other comparisons?

You probably want to know exactly what is not going well (or what is going completely wrong) in your life? Work carefully through the following pages. It's all about examining your conscience.

2.
IN & OUT

A different kind of "confession mirror"

If you want to examine your conscience – at the end of the day, or on holiday, or because you want to go to confession now – a so-called "confession mirror" can often help. Of course, nothing surpasses the Ten Commandments and the Lord's commandment to love God and love one's neighbour. You can find them inside the back cover of this book. You can find a detailed "confession mirror" in the new *Praise be to God* book (no. 599) and another in the YOUCAT book.

Here is a "confession mirror" in the form of an **IN & OUT** list. These lists are mostly a matter of taste. What's *in* today, is *out* tomorrow. Here is an **IN & OUT** list that can provide a few pointers. The most important word in this "confession mirror" is "love". Love is always *in* – it was yesterday, is today and will be tomorrow. Without love everything falls apart: the state, family, your own life. Whoever loves is directly on the way to God who is nothing but Love.

This **IN & OUT** list is a "confession mirror" which doesn't just list sins. Under *in* you will really find the things that are most in fashion. Loving, passionately seeking good and improving every day is a thousand times more important than constantly fixating on sins (*out*) for fear of making mistakes. You should be the one who loves a lot, rather than the one who is trying to avoid sin at all costs.

FOR GOD

IN

Giving God the first place in your life

Coming out as a Christian

Keeping a crucifix, an icon, a biblical poster, a sign of your faith in your room

Thinking about God first thing in the morning and last thing at night

Going to mass on Sundays

Defending God when others complain about him

Calling on God, asking him to come into your life

Looking for God and his will in the bible and in the Church

Informing yourself about your faith, educating yourself

Examining your conscience every day, going to confession regularly

OUT

Postponing your relationship with God until later

Considering yourself the greatest of all

Loving someone or something more than God

"Taking a break" from God on holiday

Being superstitious, wavering, believing in horoscopes

Escapism, having no time for God

Being ashamed of one's faith

Blaspheming against God, swearing, challenging him

Spreading gossip against the Church without checking the facts

Considering oneself better (or worse) than other sinners in front of God

VE

IN

Enjoying life

Thanking God for what's beautiful but also for what's difficult in life

Becoming involved in politics, in society, in the church. Taking responsibility for others.

Being aware, reading newspapers, watching the news, studying news portals, writing critical letters to the editor, posting on news forums

Singing, dancing, doing sport

Cooking something special and sharing it with others

Going out into nature

Making the world more homely

Appreciating creation, gazing in wonder at the stars in heaven

Listening to music and making music yourself

Eating chocolate

OUT

Living purely for one's own pleasure

Leaving the world to its own fate

Only eating junk food and producing ever more plastic waste

Only working for your own purse

Not resisting greed

Spoiling the environment

Being cruel to animals

Exploiting the land, the labour, the love of others, exploiting one's own body

Hiding, burying one's talents and gifts

Being lazy, allowing things to rot

Moaning, criticising everything, being pessimistic

IN

Being grateful

Forgiving others from
the heart and asking for
forgiveness oneself

Making others happy

Patiently tolerating those who
are difficult

Acting nobly, being
"honourable" and idealistic

Praying for others

Calling injustice by its name

Helping older people and
people with learning difficulties

Rejoicing with others, feeling
compassion for others

Acting on behalf of outsiders

Treating those of the other sex
with respect

Being honest,
not hurting others

Being 100% faithful

OUT

Being malicious, gossiping,
wearing others down

Taking intellectual property
from the internet

Deceiving, tricking, lying, being
false and spinning webs

Manipulating others, using
others for your own ends

Spreading other's secrets

Looking down on others

Leading someone astray,
using someone sexually

Envying others

Saying nothing when my friends
take drugs

Making false promises

Being unforgiving, not wanting
to recognise your own mistakes

Being a danger to others
on the road

Collaborating in or agreeing
to an abortion

FOR MYSELF

IN

OUT

Growing in faith, creating a true relationship with God

Never stopping working on oneself, educating oneself, becoming a better person

Recognising one's own strengths/weaknesses

Accepting yourself as God accepts you, looking at yourself in a positive light

Looking after one's body with care, with sun, fresh air and movement

Being able to wait until marriage

Being able to laugh at yourself, not taking yourself too seriously

Forgiving yourself

Enjoying food

Not complaining about everything

Deciding between what's important and what's not

Taking care of one's conscience

Neglecting symptoms, not going to the doctor

Being fanatical about the way you look

Smoking, taking drugs, getting drunk

Viewing pornographic images, masturbating

Making everything subordinate to one's own career

Looking for pity

Suppressing and playing down addictions and dependencies

Exploiting one's body, extreme overworking

Carelessly putting your life at risk

Being selfish

Letting yourself be ruled by bad habits

THE SACRAMENT OF PENANCE

How does it work?
What do you need?
Just how do you
do it?

First of all you need

Contrition.

This means that you are really sorry. It's not enough just to pay lip service to something just because you read somewhere that this or that is a sin.

You need to be convinced that you have done something wrong, that you have hurt or sullied yourself or others, that you forgot God and have messed up the divine order. Your conscience is left hanging when it is not orientated towards the Commandments. (You can find the "Ten Commandments" and the "Lord's Commandment" inside the back cover of the book). Before you switch on your conscience, you need to know "you must not lie". (Eighth Commandment).

But be careful. We like to deceive ourselves and say, "Hey, I'll sort that out with my conscience! I'll take responsibility for that!"

People have lied, betrayed and murdered with reference to their conscience. So, if you are unsure about anything, ask the priest. He can help you to balance your conscience against God's commandments.

→ 1 Jn 1:8

→ 297
Can a person form their conscience?

You also need Purpose of Amendment for

True Contrition.

> **"** You may fall, but not to get up again is unforgivable.
>
> WINSTON CHURCHILL

This means you really need to have the intention not to recommit the sins that you confess to the priest.

Now you might say, "That's impossible! I know full well that I'll turn to drugs again. I just won't manage." That's you being realistic. You might not manage to say goodbye to drugs immediately but if you really have the intention to do so and really want to give it your best shot, you can be sure that God will grant you forgiveness and peace through the service of the priest. You will see. You receive a supernatural power for good at confession which we call "grace". Perhaps you will be overcome by the urge to do wrong one day and you won't be able to resist the temptation. Simply go back to confession again. You can go back a thousand times with the same story. It won't make any difference to God's mercy, not at all.

→ Lk 15:11–32

He is always the Father with open arms and he has prepared a feast for you again. You don't believe me? It's true!

Then you will also need

To Confess.

This means that it's not enough to keep a collection of sins and omissions in your heart that you just beam up quickly once a week between getting undressed and falling asleep. It's important to do a small examination of conscience regularly.

If you really want to be fully reconciled with God (or need to be because you have committed a grave sin which is separating you from God), the only thing that helps is confessing to a priest.

Jesus gave the apostles and their followers an almost unbelievable power when he said, "Those whose sins you forgive, they will be forgiven. Those whose sins you retain, they will be retained." Only God can forgive sins. Jesus Christ entrusts this miracle to the Church. God's love wanted things to be concrete. If you really want to start again in your life stop sending self-reproaches up to heaven. Just go to a priest and say, "This is how it is. I repent before God." If the priest sees that you really mean it, he will grant you God's forgiveness.

→ Jn 20:23

  → 228
Who can
forgive sins?

Read more
under
Questions about
Confession on
"serious" sins
(p. 81) and the
power to forgive
sins (p. 73)

COME RIGHT IN!

Or, The Rite of Confession

Let's just assume you opted for the confessional rather than a face-to-face confession*. You examined your conscience beforehand and maybe you also wrote a confession note**. You asked God the Holy Spirit to grant you a good confession***. OK then! The green light outside the confessional is on (or there's another sign indicating that no one else is confessing at that moment), so you go in.

The priest greets you. Now it's your turn. You make the sign of the cross saying:

In the name of the Father and of the Son and of the Holy Spirit. Amen.

The priest then says the following or similar words:

May God, who has enlightened every heart, help you to know your sins and trust in his mercy.

to which you reply:

Amen.

Easy!

You now have time to confess your sins, time to "accuse yourself". It sounds harsh but that's what it means. You should confess your guilt rather than state your innocence. So, it's a proper personal accusation. Wow, that takes courage.

Simply say what you realised when you examined your life in front of God. There are two fundamental questions to ask yourself, both equally important. The first is:

What **wrong** have I **done**?

And the second is:

Where have I **failed to do good**?

Here's a small tip. Sometimes we sin more by what we don't do than what we do, just in case you can't think of where you have sinned.

You can take your confession note** with you if it helps.

At the end of your confession you say something that expresses your contrition, for example:

Those are my sins.
I acknowledge them humbly and with remorse.

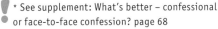 * See supplement: What's better – confessional or face-to-face confession? page 68
** find out more on page 51
*** take a look at a few prayers for confession, page 35

Now it's the priest's turn!

He may ask you a question but he'll do so with great care and courtesy. The priest isn't trying to catch you out. It is *your* confession and the confessor is offering you a divine ministry. He wants to help you to acknowledge your sins and put them into words.

He then gives you some spiritual advice which means he says things to you which may help you.

The priest then gives you a small "penance" which is usually a prayer to be said after confession. This represents a small sign of your

Repentance

and your intention to

Make reparation

for having offended God with your sin. This reparation is a component of the sacrament of penance and this also means repairing any damage you have caused to the best of your ability. If you have stolen something, you need to give it back (even if you do so anonymously). If you have hurt someone, you need to at least apologise to them.

That's when the priest can grant you

Absolution

God, the Father of mercies,
through the death and resurrection of his Son
has reconciled the world to himself
and sent the Holy Spirit among us for the forgiveness
of sins.
Through the ministry of the Church
may God give you pardon and peace,
and I absolve you from your sins
in the name of the Father ✠ and of the Son
and of the Holy Spirit.

Your response is: *Amen*.

To conclude the priest says:

The Lord has freed you from your sins. Go in peace.

SPECIAL PRAYERS
FOR CONFESSION

Many people think that sins and confession are all about talking to yourself a lot. Not true. It is better to light a candle, talk to God, or gaze at a crucifix or an icon. A lot becomes clear about yourself when you dialogue with God. A good confession is always accompanied by special prayers. You may want to pray using your own words or you may want to use these prayers:

Wash me more and more from my guilt

And cleanse me from my sin.
My offenses truly I know them
My sin is always before me.
Against you, you alone have I sinned,
What is evil in your sight I have done.
Wash me, I shall be whiter than snow.
Make me hear rejoicing and gladness
That the bones you have crushed may revive
Do not cast me away from your presence
Nor deprive me of your holy spirit.
Give me again the joy of your help
With a spirit of fervour sustain me.
Amen.

From PSALM 51

A prayer for a good examination of conscience

Come, O my dear Lord,

and teach me in the like manner.

And, for that end, give me, O my Lord,
that purity of conscience
which alone can receive,
which alone can improve Thy inspirations.
My ears are dull,
so that I cannot hear Thy voice.
My eyes are dim,
so that I cannot see Thy tokens.
Thou alone canst quicken my hearing,
and purge my sight,
and cleanse and renew my heart.
Teach me, like Mary, to sit at Thy feet,
and hear Thy word. Amen

JOHN HENRY NEWMAN

A prayer to the Holy Spirit for a good confession

Come, Holy Spirit,

Give me the grace to recognise my sins exactly
that I may truly repent of them
that I may confess them honestly and sincerely
And genuinely improve. Amen.

Acts of contrition

O my God,

I am truly sorry
that I have responded so poorly
to your love for me
It hurts deep within my soul
that I have sinned
in my words,
my thoughts, my actions and omissions
against your never-ending mercy.
Forgive me, Lord.
Look kindly on me as I come to you,
imperfect and with empty hands.
Have mercy on me.
I believe that you want to welcome me
back as your child.
I seek your love and your boundless forgiveness.
I firmly resolve to do penance,
not to sin again
and to avoid the occasions for sin.
Cure me
through your suffering and dying
and give me the grace
to respond better to your love.
Amen.

Jesus,

I'm sorry
that I failed to love you again.
The temptation was often so great
and I myself too weak
or my trust in you too small.
I thank you
for wanting to forgive me again and again
and, strengthened by this confession,
I promise to take up
the challenge again to live a new life,
a life that pleases you.

I ask you to give me strength for all the battles
that await me, and make me aware
that you are always with me.
I am happy that you count on me
and still have so much planned for me.
Let me not be discouraged, my God,
by the disappointments
that I cause You.
Amen.

RUDOLF GEHRIG

How beautiful

it is, good Father,
that we cannot fall out of your hands.
They are beneath us when we fall;
They are beside us when we waver;
They are above us in danger.

BERNHARD MEUSER

Oh God,

When I stumble over all the hurdles
and fall under the weight of the trials
and collapse in every situation
and am finally counted out
because I fail to get up,
there I find You at the bottom of the pit
with me and in my faith.

BERNHARD MEUSER

Help me, Lord,

to know you more clearly,
love you more dearly
and follow you more nearly.

IGNATIUS OF LOYOLA

My Lord and My God,

Take from me everything that keeps me from You.
My Lord and my God, give everything to me that
brings me near to You. My Lord and my God,
take me away from myself and give me completely
to You.

NIKLAUS VON DER FLÜE

Father,

I abandon myself into your hands. Do with me
what you will. Whatever you may do, I thank you:
I am ready for all, I accept all. Let only your will
be done in me, and in all your creatures – I wish
no more than this, O Lord. Into your hands I
commend my soul: I offer it to you with all the love
of my heart, for I love you, Lord, and so need to
give myself, to surrender myself into your hands
without reserve, and with boundless confidence,
for you are my Father.

CHARLES DE FOUCAULD

3.
CONFESS? YES, I CAN!

Rudolf Gehrig, 19, has finished his exams. He is currently volunteering in the parish of Senden, in Bavaria, to understand what God wants for his life. "Confession" has become an important part of his life since the last World Youth Day.

It was only meant to be a simple prank. I fired one of those large rubber bands across the classroom but it hit the glass on the door then landed right in the teacher's face. I was consequently reprimanded and had to go through the school playground at every break time picking up rubbish with a big rubbish bag and tongs. Great!! Have you any idea how much chewing-gum a playground of that size holds? Well, I do. Anyway, one break wasn't enough to clean up the whole playground, and even the places that I had cleaned up were just as bad again the following day.

Too much rubbish in my life

A banana peel can take approximately one year to decompose, depending on the condition of the soil and the level of humidity, a plastic bag can take between 1,000 and 3,000 years, and uranium 238 only reduces to half its size after 4,468 hundred thousand years. Yet that's nothing compared to the rubbish that never rots away - sin. At a certain point in my life I understood that sin produces a particular type of rubbish that can be classified as "highly toxic" because it affects everyone and can affect

and destroy our life. It makes my inner landscape filthy. Sin has no half-life, it doesn't decompose but there is a way of getting rid of all this rubbish – through confession.

Start Again!

Confession is really quite simple. This much I know. God says to me, "Yes, you have sinned but because you are truly sorry and because I love you, I forgive you". He rips up all my debts, presses the Reset button, empties the Recycle Bin and clicks Restart, giving me another opportunity to make a new start.

I don't actually go "right back to the beginning". It's not like in Ludo where the little figure has to go right back to the beginning and do the whole journey again. It's more like with a Carrera race track. I start going off track because of all the sins that have built up over time. God takes my car and puts it back on the race track. I don't have to go right back to the beginning. I just carry on from where I went off track. I'm back in the race again, all cleaned up with a full tank. Hey, from now on I'm driving with a new set of tyres.

Whatever our hearts condemn, God is greater than our hearts and knows everything.

1 JN 3:20

→ 314

How do we know that God is merciful?

It's not what I want but it just keeps happening.

Ever since the Fall of Adam and Eve, well, that's just the way it is. The thing with sin is that it keeps happening no matter how hard I try to fight it. If I ever got to the point where I can say, "Yes! I've made it. I know I'll never sin again", I would either be dead or so blinded by arrogance that it would really be high time I went to confession.

→ 68
Original sin? What does the Fall of Adam and Eve have to do with us?

How was your day?

Every evening before I go to sleep I get into a conversation with God. God asks me, "Hey son, what good did you do today? Where did you mess up?" That way I stop certain sins becoming a habit and slowly deadening my conscience. C S Lewis once compared the conscience to a sharp stone in the heart. The stone pierces your heart each time you sin but if you keep sinning, the stone is in constant contact with the wall of your heart, and eventually your heart starts to form such a tough skin that you don't even notice that you are sinning.

" The most uncomfortable way to go forward is looking at yourself.

KARL RAHNER

I need an early warning system

With some things I know immediately when I am on the wrong track. With others I don't realise what's happening but here too the priest to whom I confess (my "confessor") has helped me to see clearly on more than one occasion. I have also learned a lot through reading the Holy Scriptures or leafing through the catechism.

I have seen how easily it is to end up on the wrong track.

→ 312
How does someone know that they have sinned?

Love begins today. Today someone is suffering. Today someone is on the streets. Today someone is hungry. Today we have to commit. Yesterday is gone. Tomorrow has not yet come. We only have today to make God known by loving, serving, feeding the hungry, clothing the naked, finding shelter for the poor. Don't wait until tomorrow! They will be dead tomorrow if we don't give them something today.
MOTHER TERESA

I hit my little brother. I really hadn't meant to. He's normally a nice lad. So, what happened? Well there was this thing with the two Euros which were lying on my desk and suddenly disappeared. My brother denies it and empties his piggy bank to prove he hasn't taken the two Euros but I'm not that convinced of his innocence. Then he takes the last bread roll at breakfast even though I'm still really hungry but out of love hold back to see if mum or dad want it.

My little brother gets away with everything. They never tell him off. I feel offended as I watch how he proudly shows our parents the picture he'd painted and how mum sticks it straight on the fridge-door. Then he comes into my room three times without knocking and when I catch him with my mobile after he's looked at all my text messages, I just hit him. He then goes crying to mum, my hand stings and I suddenly feel really bad. Why did I get annoyed, I ask you?

In your anger do not sin! Do not let the sun go down while you are still angry.
EP 4:26

I realise it's often the little things that turn into disasters. Having an early warning system helps. I can take precautions and avoid certain occasions for sin. For example, if I know it's better for me not to take my PC into the bedroom, then I leave it outside. This is better than having to kneel before God the next morning and ask him to forgive me because I've been surfing through the murky waters of the Internet until the early hours of the morning.

" Temptations are like vagabonds: if you treat them kindly, they come back and bring others with them.
DWIGHT L. MOODY

I must also want it!

A friend of mine who clearly enjoys his food starts quite a strict diet, six weeks before Christmas and manages to keep it up for five weeks. Then a parcel arrives from his aunt. It sits on the table for a while. He knows exactly what's in it - a whole load of homemade biscuits. My friend knows that as soon as he opens the parcel and sees the biscuits he's going to scoff the lot as he won't be able to resist. He looks at the parcel again, suddenly decides to open it anyway, and that's the end of his diet.

99 Do what you can do and pray for his aid for what you cannot do.

SAINT AUGUSTINE

 → **291**

How can a person tell whether their action is good or bad?

It's no use having an early warning system if I have no willpower. I need more than just common sense to resist the destructive power of sin in my life. I need a healthy dose of *willpower* and sound judgment to be able to distinguish between good and bad.

A little plug
for the "confession note"

Yeah, yeah. I know you shouldn't have to write down your sins if you want to go to confession. No-one who regularly receives the sacrament of reconciliation with God does that. Well, someone once said to me "a *confession note* and a *"confession mirror"* are like the left and right crutch for a good confession. Once you've learned how to walk you can throw them out." I haven't got that far yet so I'll keep using them for as long as I need to. I really want to take my relationship with God seriously.

A "confession mirror" really helps me. Without it, I only know that I haven't killed anyone or robbed a bank which is already a great start but I need "the list" to remind me that it's not just about the *bad* things that I didn't do. It's also about the times where I really messed up – the *good* things that I failed to do for God, for others and for myself.

99 Our dear Lord loves being disturbed.

JEAN MARIE
VIANNEY
(CURE D'ARS)

Working on my list of faults

I use a "confession mirror" because I'm still 'in training'. I go through it point by point in the same way that train inspectors use a checklist to inspect high-speed train carriages. I transfer the relevant points to my "list of faults". The feeling of shock that I get when I reach the end of a long list of faults is already the "contrition" I need if I want God to forgive my sins. The "tough nuts" are at the top of my list so that I can get them out of the way quickly at confession and am not tempted to leave them out because I feel so embarrassed about them.

Rip! Rip! Rip!

The thing with the confession note is that it's particularly symbolic. Once it has served its purpose, I tear it up into tiny little pieces – rip, rip,

99 Don't complain about what can't be changed, but change the things you complain about.

WILLIAM SHAKESPEARE

99 To recognise the will of God you need three things – prayer, patience and counsel.

JOHN BOSCO

rip. It's as if everything that stood between me and God has been blown away. Just read what Paul wrote in his letter to the Colossians. "He (Christ) has obliterated the bond against us."

→ Col 2:14

One other thing. I don't share my confession note by text, nor post it on Facebook or scribble it in my maths book. I simply take some paper and write my confession note, at the earliest the day before confession. Immediately after the absolution all that remains are tiny scraps blown away by the wind or consumed by the flames.

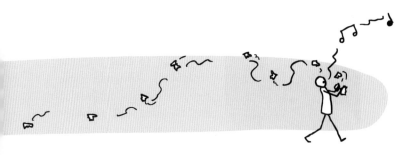

STOP!

What matters most is Love!

Many people overdo it when they examine their conscience. Their Christian life and their prayer life consist in frantically looking for new sins that they might have committed. They think God will only love them if they make themselves as small and as bad as they can in front of him. They stop living life to the full. They don't dare to do anything in case they do something wrong. Instead of praising God's greatness, all they can think about are their own weaknesses. They're constantly telling God what terrible sinners they are.

These people are called *scrupulous* ("scruples" = false inhibitions). A well-known confessor, the French Curé d'Ars, Jean Marie Vianney (1786-1859) often had to deal with the scrupulous. Anyone who went to him for confession had to avoid "all pointless self-accusations, all those scruples repeated over again which waste the confessor's time and annoy everyone waiting at the confessional."

The Curé d'Ars recommended *"confessing what was uncertain as uncertain, and what was certain as certain." What mattered to him was "that nothing should be false. Speak from the heart. You might be able to fool your confessor but you can never fool our dear Lord."*

What's clear is that an examination of conscience needs to be made again and again but please keep it *short, clear and to the point!* The Cure d'Ars preferred short, honest, succinct confessions.

+ God forgives and "forgets" sins.
+ So, you need to forget them too.
+ Stop fixating on the sin
+ Look at God who is Love.

Christians should be recognised by their joy.

God doesn't want you to walk around like the depressed types who continually look at the abyss of their own soul.

BERNHARD MEUSER

Hmmm...

→ 228

Who can
forgive sins?

→ 238

Can a priest
later repeat
something he
has heard
in confession?

I'm looking for a priest.

I know, many people would rather get rid of their sins directly through night prayers to Jesus, or pour out their hearts to their best friend and be absolved by a machine but Jesus gave the Church the authority to forgive sins. Jesus sets the rules of the game. I believe him and look for a priest so that I can start again. Although you might not be able to take your old glass to the recycling depot after hours, you can always go to a priest within reason, unless it's an emergency. (Aeroplane about to crash, priest in front of me sleeping like a log. Should I wake him?) Every parish has its own times for confession. I can look them up on the internet, in the parish newsletter or ask the parish priest.

I have asked myself whether it's better to confess to a priest that I know well or to go to someone who doesn't know me at all. I do both but slightly prefer the second option. Both of us need to be careful not to act as if the sacrament hadn't been present were the walls between us to come down for a moment.

How often do I go to confession? The rule is clear to me. Anyone who has committed a serious sin should go to confession and may not receive communion until they have done so. Otherwise every Catholic should go to confession once a year, especially before Easter, even if they are not aware of having committed any serious sins. How often do I go? A few times a year. I ought to go more often but there is a little devil who sometimes scuppers my plans.

 Confessional or face-to-face confession – what's better? Page 68

→ 234

When is a Catholic obliged to confess their serious sins? How often should one go to confession?

Don't get hung up on it!

99 Remember that before you reach the Promised Land you have to cross the Red Sea and the desert.
DON JOHN BOSCO

I can suddenly think of a thousand reasons not to keep my appointment with HIM in the confessional. I suddenly remember that I need to clean out the rabbit hutch or that I haven't called my friend back or that the carburettor on my moped needs changing urgently. Or I suddenly decide that I'm not as bad as I thought, that my sins are my business not my priest's and that I'm embarrassed to have ever believed in this nonsense about forgiveness of sins and writing confession notes. OK, I don't want to shirk my responsibilities but there is someone at work on the other side who really doesn't like me being reconciled with God. I get butterflies, break out in a sweat, my heart races, blood pressure goes up, bladder problems? Off to the doctor's! Or off to the confessional. It's now or never! Before I rush into the confessional, I pause for a minute to speak with God. I ask him for a good confession. Once in the confessional I shut the door behind me. My heart seems

! You can **●** find special prayers to prepare for confession on pages 35 to 41.

to beat faster than it did on my first date. No wonder. After all I am meeting someone who is more powerful and impressive that anyone else on this earth.

The priest is only "the ear".

After the introduction, off I go. I just say everything! I work through my confession note, point by point. Sometimes I just use the note as a prompt. The priest is listening to me in Jesus's place. He is "the ear", everything else is secondary. I am speaking to Jesus. He knows me and he is not surprised when I pull out another bag of rubbish I had almost forgotten about from the corner of my heart. He also knows about the dark parts of my soul, and he is pleased that I am finally letting in light. When I have told Jesus my sins I make an act of contrition. It's nothing complicated. It simply means that I add an "I'm sorry" to the "I broke the window". It's enough to say, "Those are my sins. I acknowledge them and am sorry"

Details of how to make a confession can be found on pages 30 to 33.

→ 232
What must I bring to the confession?

99 Forgiveness is not something you do once. It is a lifestyle.
MARTIN LUTHER KING JR.

→ 314
How do we know that God is merciful?

99 For those who love God, He changes everything into good. He even allows our faults and mistakes to be changed into good.
SAINT AUGUSTINE

It took me a while to understand that God is not in the least bit angry with me because of my sins. He knows that I am a weak creature. There's no need for me to put on the look of innocence to soften his heart or pacify him. My sins make God sad, not angry. I imagine how pleased he is that I am wholeheartedly sorry and asking him for forgiveness. Contrition is so important, otherwise I might as well not go to confession.

In the history of humankind, God has never turned away anyone who has asked for forgiveness. Maybe not what you'd expect if you thought about how you'd react if your friend kept making a mess of everything. He apologises, you forgive him then he does it again. At a certain point you'll have had enough of it.

Not God.

It's already been paid

Just imagine. I'm standing in the bank with a list of debts. I go to the counter. A nice man with a smart tie is sitting there. My whole body shakes while he goes through my debts. Then I confess to him that regrettably I can't pay off any of my debts. I'm at the end of my tether. What does he do, the man at the counter? He looks up, gazes kindly into my eyes then rips up my list of debts into tiny pieces. "It doesn't matter," he says, "it's already been paid."

> God is more prepared to forgive a contrite sinner than a mother is to save her child from the fire.
>
> JEAN MARIE VIANNEY (CURE D'ARS)

→ **Eph 2:8–9**

That's how confession works. "It's already been paid." Jesus has paid for me! Yes, it is hard to understand but two thousand years ago God actually decided to pay for our sins. When a company pays for a team's football shirts, the company boss will naturally expect the footballers to wear the company logo on their shirts to increase the company's profile and profits. God thinks differently and does so out of love. God is Love and love is unconditional and doesn't seek its own interests.

→ 337
How are we saved?

Though your sins be like scarlet, they may become white as snow. Though they be crimson red, they may become white as wool.

IS 1:18

The priest is the man at the counter of life, ready to tear up my list of debts on God's behalf. It is sad to see how many people run around outside in despair, using the wildest methods and absurd, alleged "miracle cures" to get rid of their list of debts instead of going to the man at the counter and letting him tear it up.

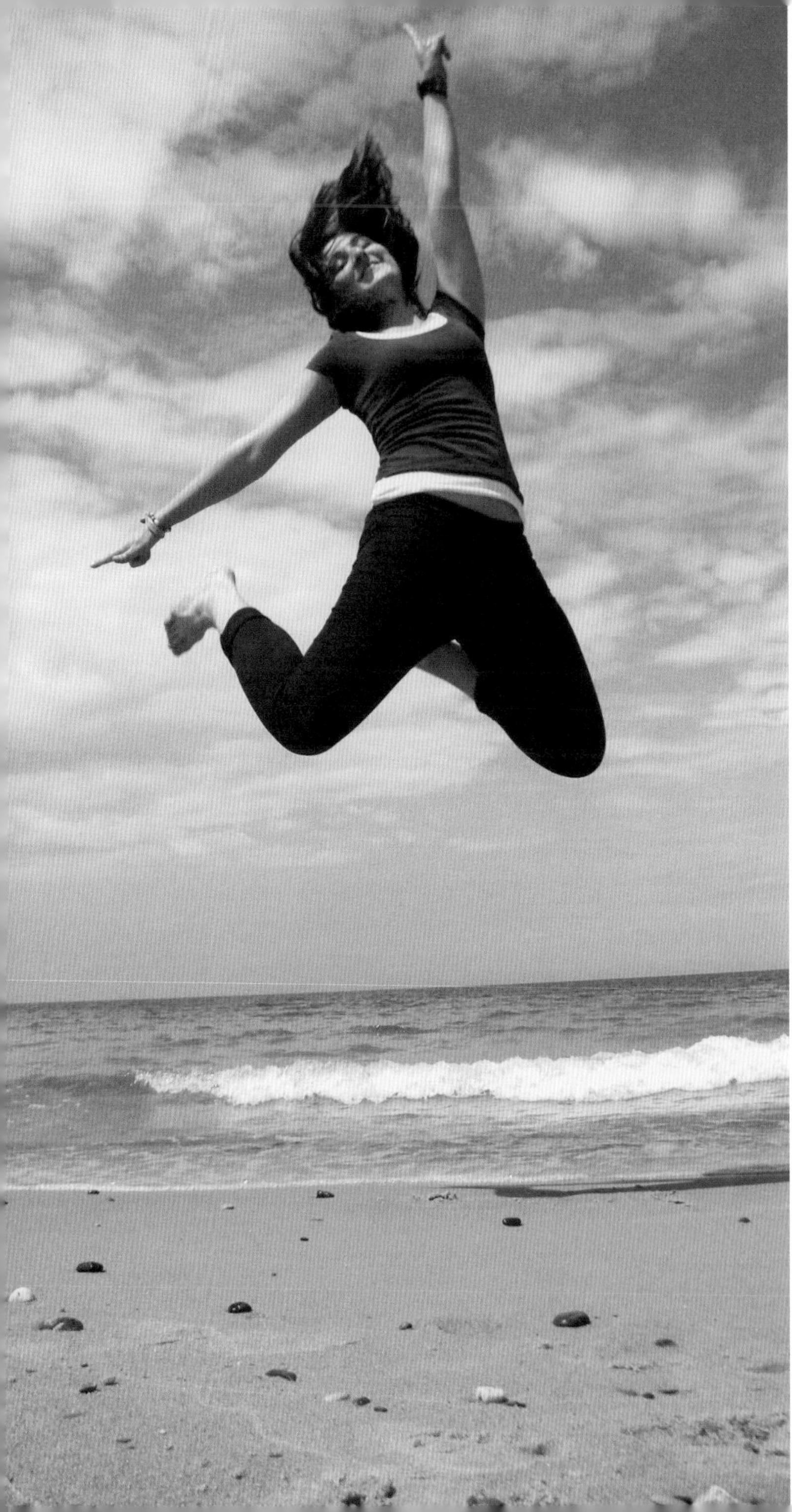

Another great story

99 Jesus in the confessional is not a coin-operated launderette.
It is a meeting with Jesus. He is waiting for us and accepts us just as we are.

POPE FRANCIS

I once heard this cool story. There was a man who had been through a lot in his life and had totally distanced himself from God. One day for 'fun' he decided to go to confession and play a joke on the priest. He told him all his wild stories then declared at the end of it all scornfully he wasn't a bit sorry and made fun of the priest's apparent naivete.

The priest couldn't absolve him of his sins of course but he said to the young man, "If you really feel that way, go to the crypt and stand in front of the crucifix. Then look at Jesus and say ten times out loud, "I don't care that you died for me." Struck by his dignity, the man did indeed follow the priest's instructions. He went into the crypt, stood in front of the crucifix and said, "I don't care that you died for me." He repeated the phrase a few more times. Suddenly he broke

down in tears and threw himself to the ground. He went back once again into the confessional. This time he made a proper confession, and this time he was absolved for his sins and was converted from then on. He had been touched by the love of God.

The priest is only God's tool. He couldn't absolve the young man of his past at first because it was clear that he felt no remorse for his sins. To be truly remorseful, you need to want to avoid sin and change your behaviour. Of course, it is difficult to change your behaviour and completely refrain from doing wrong in the future, but I should at least try. God will help me. After the absolution you receive a penance from the priest which is usually a prayer. Many people think of "penance" as a kind of gruesome punishment that the church has devised to intimidate the people. It's more about giving God *a sign of reparation and gratitude* which shows my willingness to make up for the damage done.

99 There is no moment in our life when we can't beat a new path.
CHARLES DE FOUCAULD

→ 230
What is penance?

99 Sins against the sixth commandment are by no means the worst but the stickiest.

THOMAS AQUINAS

I once went to confession with a priest from South Tirol, and we were having such a good chat that he forgot in the end what penance he was going to give me. He gave me quite a shock when he said, "OK then, for your penance please climb Mount Everest on your knees." In the end, thanks be to God, he reduced it to a prayer.

After confession

→ 339

What does God's grace do to us?

I feel enormously happy, liberated! There have been moments when I have cried tears of joy after confession but also moments where I haven't felt anything. I asked a priest if I had done something wrong. He said to me, "You haven't done anything wrong. Your confession worked. In the sacrament of reconciliation, it's not a question of *feeling* that your sins have been forgiven but *knowing* that they have been forgiven. If you also feel something after confession that's even better!" Phew. That was such a relief.

What if I fall back into my old ways?

I can keep falling flat on my face as long as I keep picking myself up again to carry on the fight. In a moment of carelessness, I have been caught off guard in the boxing ring with the devil and get one right on the nose. It's not serious if I fall to the ground in those moments. The referee starts counting down, and I get back onto my feet! So, it makes absolutely no difference how many times I fall, as long as I love the fight and keep getting up again.

I will win because I believe in God and he believes in me.

Then Jesus said to the adulteress, "Neither do I judge you. Go and sin no more."

JN 8:11

Confessional or face-to-face confession?

What's better?

The **Confessional** allows you to remain largely anonymous, where the confessor is more the judge, rather than the understanding friend and counsellor who listens to you patiently and enters into a conversation with you. He hears your confession, takes your contrition seriously then absolves you of your sins.

It's important to know that it makes no difference whether the priest hearing your confession is a holy man or someone who is struggling personally or in his own life when it comes to how he serves you. He would still absolve you of your sins under the authority of Christ even if he were a criminal. Let's be honest. We often expect the priest to minimise our sins when we're having an understanding discussion by saying, "Look, it's not that serious!" It annoys me when a priest says something like that. I am standing before God and if my conscience is pricking me I don't want to hear, "Oh, you poor thing. You must have had a terrible childhood!"

I myself normally use the confessional, once a month usually. I go well prepared and the whole thing doesn't take long – five to seven minutes as a rule. In those moments where I prefer a more detailed discussion about my life, then the confessional is not the appropriate space. On those occasions I'll meet with the priest in his office and when I've shared everything with him, he takes his stole and puts it around his neck – the moment when he can administer the sacrament of penance – and we close the open discussion with a formal confession.

One difficulty that may arise with the confessional is that you just talk down a few sins. You quickly say a few standard sins, make the sign of the cross then go back to your everyday life. The advantage of the confessional is that you remain anonymous but whether you're in the confessional or having a face-to-face confession, what you confess remains completely confidential.

A friend recently told me about a confession in Washington. He went into a confessional in the

cathedral. A green light indicated that a priest was waiting for the next candidate. It was dark in the confessional so he couldn't see the priest's face behind the grill. My friend started giving a detailed account of his situation, how long he had been married, how many children he had, what he did for a living and what was on his mind. Suddenly a loud deep voice boomed out of the confessional, "No stories, please. Just confess." A wonderful story. I can sympathise with the man of God in Washington. It is better to get straight to the point in confession rather than beating about the bush. If you aren't sure about something or other, ask. The confessional is not a divine information booth or a psychotherapist's couch. It's the place where I meet God through his servants.

Having a **face-to-face confession** is a wonderful way to feel God's love and mercy. I have a few images in my mind. Every week at Taizé, which I have often visited, there is the "night of lights". As evening falls, various religious brothers take up position under the arcades. You can talk about your life and your vocation with some. Those wearing stoles are Catholic priests whom you can approach to ask them to hear your confession. There is often a long queue of young people waiting to receive the sacrament of reconciliation. It's almost contagious, pulling you in with the thought, "Hey, you really ought to get your life with God back in order." It's a space that is full of yearning, peace and beauty. God is at work here. He changes people in the depths of their heart.

A face-to-face confession is a wonderful thing because when you are still not sure what sin actually is or when you want to combine your return to God with a request for "directions", you simply need time and an opportunity to talk with someone who will listen with divine patience and offer help according to the Word of God.

A face-to-face confession, however, can hide a certain danger in that the whole thing could end up simply being a chat, and the priest could simply be that nice bloke that's so easy to talk to. The confession is something sacred and not to be trivialised.

BERNHARD MEUSER

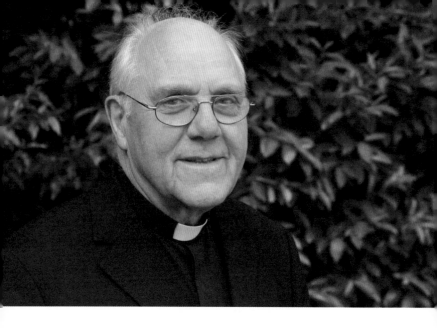

Questions about Confession

Everything you ever wanted to know

*Many young people from Cologne and the surrounding areas have a very special confessor, **Auxiliary Bishop Klaus Dick** (*1928). This kind, elderly priest who is already retired has become the confidant for people 60 years younger than him. This is a gift for both parties. The young people love his fatherly approach which makes it easy for them to be open with him. It's no wonder that young people see him as their spiritual guide. Rudolf Gehrig asked him everything he wanted to know about confession.*

YOUCAT: If you had to describe the sacrament of penance in one word, what would you say?

Auxiliary Bishop Dr Dick: the sacrament of penance is the gift of the Risen Lord to his disciples.

Sorry, I don't understand "gift of the Risen Lord"?

Just think about it. What happened on Easter Sunday when Jesus appeared to his disciples? He wished them peace, gave them the Holy Spirit and said something unbelievable, "Those whose sins you forgive, they are forgiven". The apostles conferred the "gift of the Risen Lord" to their followers, the bishops. This gift has been passed on in this way through the ordination of bishops from one generation to the next right up to the present time. The bishop confers this authority to his priests, and whenever a Christian receives the sacrament of penance through a priest or bishop, whether this be in New York or the Indonesian jungle, he receives this gift from Jesus.

→ Jn 20:23

Confession, you said, is a sacrament. What do you mean by that?

Yes, confession (or rather the sacrament of reconciliation) is one of the seven sacraments in the Catholic Church. Sacraments are holy signs introduced by God which do exactly what they are meant to. That means that you can be quite sure that your sins really are forgiven through the power of God when the priest utters the absolution. The first time a person receives forgiveness for their sins is at baptism. The first Christians were really alarmed to discover that even someone who had been baptised could sin again but through the words of Jesus they understood that sins could also be forgiven after baptism.

Someone once said to me that the Church invented confession just to keep the people under control

I think this is ridiculous. Confession is rooted in the Bible. The call to "Repent!" can be found early on in the Gospels (*Mt* 3:2: *Mk* 1:15) and our Lord Jesus Christ gave his Church the authority for this conversion with the words, "Those whose sins you forgive, they are forgiven."

How did that develop into confession in the Church?

In the beginning people believed that if they were baptised they were free from all sin and they simply didn't sin any more but they soon saw that it did still happen. They then thought they could only be forgiven once after baptism. Later it became the practice for so-called "capital sins", such as apostasy, murder and adultery, to be announced publicly before sins could be forgiven. Only later was it understood that sins could be brought to this sacrament again and again which is why a Catholic now comes to a priest individually and confesses their sins to him. The "seal of confession" was also understood at that time, but the gift of the forgiveness of sins has essentially remained the same throughout history.

The sacrifice that God wants is a contrite spirit. A humble and contrite heart, O Lord, you will not spurn.
PS 51:19

The seal of confession – that sounds exciting

Yes, it is exciting. Every confessor must be prepared to die rather than pass on what has been confided to him in confession. He is also not allowed to allude to anything revealed in confession so that no one can deduce who confessed it, even indirectly.

→ 238
May a priest later repeat something he has learned in confession?

Let's say the confessor knows me. He's surely going to think badly of me when he sees me again, isn't he?

Every confessor has the deepest respect for the "penitent". He is either full of admiration for how little someone has to confess or

You cannot 'sin away' God's love.
HENRY CHRISTIAN RUST

amazed by the penitent's courage in bringing serious transgressions to the sacrament of penance. He is always happy to be able to confer God's forgiveness. Each honest confession tells the priest that he too needs to be a better Christian. The confessor must also never allow what he has heard in confession to influence his attitude towards the penitent nor can he ever refer to the contents of someone's confession outside the sacrament of confession.

Does the confessor always have to give absolution?

The priest may not withhold absolution if the penitent is truly sorry for their sins. Nor is he allowed to criticise.

If I'm really finding it difficult to express a sin, even though it weighs heavily on my mind, is there a trick to overcoming this fear?

You simply need to think "it will help me to say it," and there will be no bad consequences. It would be foolish to go to the chemist because I urgently needed medication for my heart attacks but didn't dare to tell them I had a serious heart condition. I wouldn't get what I needed. I need to remember that I am confessing before Jesus Christ. The priest is bound by the seal of confession so it makes no sense to withhold something from Jesus that he already knows anyway.

And what if I am as vague as possible about my sins?

The confessor should be able to assess the weight of the sin to some degree. Otherwise it becomes something mechanical where even a robot could theoretically give absolution. When I confess for example that I have argued with my parents then it makes a difference whether this was the first time in 20 years it has happened or whether this had been going on for 15 years. It's important to tell the confessor. You don't have to necessarily confess in such detail on the lighter sins. The confession is not a tax declaration.

99 The power of evil lives off the cowardice of the good.
JOHN BOSCO

→ 396

How does a Christian deal with anger?

How would you advise me to confess?

There are no regulations. What matters is that you examine your conscience: "What have I done wrong in front of God?" Then you need to be truly sorry and say to yourself, "Something needs to change here" and for this to happen, it's important that you express the confession. At the end of the day the priest as confessor needs to know from what he is absolving the penitent.

Why is God so interested in my sins?

God is Love. It really matters to him what we do and don't do! He is interested in our every thought and every word. Sin is what destroys us. Do you think God doesn't care if we, his beloved children keep destroying ourselves? That's why the confessor has the task of making it clear that every sin – including those committed against someone else – affects my relationship with God, and God wants to put that right again.

Does God also forgive sins that I haven't confessed?

God always forgives without limits including sins that I forgot to name in confession. To decide not to confess a sin would however indicate a lack of remorse. God cannot forgive sins for which there is no sense of remorse.

So what should I confess?

The sacrament of penance is for all sins but it is particularly important for the sins that have destroyed my relationship with God. These are the so-called

"deadly sins". It is important that these sins are confessed because a broken relationship with God must first be re-established to be able to receive the Eucharist again, for example. Everything else is a lighter sin, a so-called "venial sin". These can and should also be confessed but we are not obliged to do so by the Church.

Is confession not just an open charter that says, "Well, I'll just go and confess everything again"?

Anyone who thinks like that has not yet made a proper confession. If I make a confession without the intention to change my behaviour

 → **234**

When is a Catholic obliged to confess their serious sins? How often should one go to confession?

→ **233**

Which sins must be confessed?

afterwards, the confession is invalid. How can I expect God to forgive me? The moment I sin and say indifferently, "It's not as bad as all that. I'll just go and confess again" is itself a sin.

Why should I confess at all if I am bound to sin again anyway?

Those who confess regularly are already making the next appointment for confession. I make that commitment to avoid sin and to better myself but I know I won't manage immediately. A confession becomes very real when I know I'm going to sin again. What matters is that I use this new start that God is giving me. It may be that I plan to do something ten times and get it wrong ten times but then I get it right the eleventh time.

It's so frustrating if I confess the same thing every time...

Yes, many people say that to me to which I reply, "Do you think you need to give God a bit of variety? Do you need to sin differently sometimes?" Be happy that you always confess the same thing! One day, if you stopped confessing because you always confessed the same things, you would one day do something that was even more serious than your standard sin. I too always confess the same things."

> Glory is not found in never falling but in always getting up again.
>
> SAINT AUGUSTINE

How often should I go to confession?

Well, really there are no set rules as to how often I should go to confession except to receive the sacrament of penance at least once a year. It is helpful for those who really want to live a life with God to go to confession at regular intervals (the old recommendation was every four weeks).

→ 235
Can I make a confession even if I have not committed any serious sins?

You said something before about a "mortal sin". What exactly is that?

A mortal sin or "heavy" sin is a clear "No!" to God, where one of the commandments has been consciously and purposefully broken. Since time immemorial this has always been apostasy, murder and adultery but today we also have to add severe slander, refusing to help in an emergency, abortion, people trafficking, withdrawal of basic necessities for life, etc. What's important is that to have committed a mortal sin you need "clear awareness".

What is the difference between a serious sin and a venial sin?

I want to explain it simply with the words of a nine-year old schoolchild, "When I haven't loved God at all, that's a serious sin. When I haven't loved God enough, that's a venial sin." If you know God and still say "No" to him then you are definitely on the wrong track.

On the subject of sex. Many young people are very unsure and consider sex before marriage as normal. They want to try it out to see whether or not they make a good match ...

There is a wonderful quote from Pope John Paul II, "physical and sexual union is something wonderful and

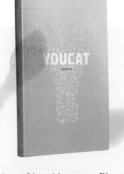

409 *Is masturbation an offence against love?*

The Church does not demonise masturbation but warns against trivialising it. In fact, many young people and adults are in danger of becoming isolated in their consumption of lewd images, films and Internet services instead of finding love in a personal relationship. Loneliness can lead to a blind alley in which masturbation becomes an addiction. Living by the motto
"I don't need anyone for sex;
I will have it for myself, however and whenever I need it"
makes nobody happy.

beautiful...You cannot try out life, nor can you try out death. You cannot try out love, nor can you try out welcoming someone into the world." Just imagine a child being conceived during such a "trial period". How often have I heard in confession, "We had to abort the child", which means kill the child. Or else they have the child but cannot live together because they are still very young and immature. What an injustice for this new life that has

→ **408**
How can you live as a young Christian if you are living in a pre-marital relationship or have already had pre-marital relationships?

come into the world longing for love! That's why the Church says that sex is something beautiful but only in its full beauty when you know you want to stay together for ever which is when you get married.

If I am in a pre-marital relationship and can't change it, can I even go to confession?

Certainly. It should definitely be brought to confession! One can say to God: "I'm sorry that I can't change it!" and consider seriously with the confessor whether and how you can correspond better to the will of God. This is when the priest can help.

Many people say "I don't need commandments. All I need is my conscience which tells me what's right and what's wrong."

If that were the case there would be no truth, no right or wrong because one person would behave according to their conscience and another, behaving according to their conscience, would do the exact opposite. One priest would consider it good what I had done and the other would consider it something bad. The conscience is the ability to distinguish between good and bad but on

the basis of the norms and commandments available. "You must not lie!" This is always true. Conscience is more profoundly the ability to apply set norms. Once I know that I mustn't lie then there are everyday situations where I have to put this into practice. In confession the priest helps me to recognise what the truth is.

How does the conscience work?

Here's an example. When a father forbids his children from running around because otherwise the expensive Chinese vase will break, they immediately have a bad conscience when the vase does get broken. If nothing had been said to the children they wouldn't have been aware of the damage they had done. That's how our conscience is formed. It is like an old pair of pharmacy scales with two weighing bowls. On the one side we have the weights (norms, commandments, words from the Bible, words of Jesus), on the other there are the facts. The more weights I have the easier it is to assess a situation, and I can see whether something is good or bad. You read the words of Jesus in the Bible: "Whatever you do to the least, that you

→ 297
Can a person form their conscience?

→ Mt 25:40

do unto me!" and you've understood immediately. Then you will never again pass by a poor person without paying them attention. The word of Jesus is a very strong weight.

How can I make sure that my conscience is as well-informed as possible?

By collecting as many weights as possible and by examining one's conscience again and again, perhaps in the evening. In this way you can avoid dangerous situations where you act against your conscience.

There is some kind of rule that says you should first go to confession if you want to receive communion. What would I need to have done for this?

Communion is the deepest union with Christ; an intimate union between Christ and each individual Christian

is unimaginable. How is this going to happen if at the same time I'm saying "No!" to God through a serious sin? The receiving of communion would just be a lie. So, whoever is burdened by a sin that is separating him from God must go and confess before receiving communion. Otherwise he receives the sacrament of the Eucharist unworthily.

After the absolution I get another "penance". That just sounds like a punishment

Yes, the word penance is very misleading. God has absolved me of my sin and that is enough. I don't then have to carry out huge penances for the absolution to work. That's why the priest usually asks that you say a small prayer – as a sign of the reparation and the gratitude towards God. Besides our willingness to repair the damage done, my joy is expressed in being able to begin a completely new life with God.

> The confessional is not a torture chamber. God is not waiting to hit me but to welcome me with gentleness.
> POPE FRANCIS

THE BASICS:

THE TEN COMMANDMENTS

1. I am the Lord, your God. You shall have no other gods beside me.
2. You shall not take the name of God in vain.
3. You shall keep holy the day of the Lord.
4. You shall honour your father and mother.
5. You shall not kill.
6. You shall not commit adultery.
7. You shall not steal.
8. You shall not bear false witness against your neighbour.
9. You shall not covet your neighbour's wife.
10. You shall not covet your neighbour's goods. → 349

THE DOUBLE COMMANDMENT OF LOVE

Which our consciences can *always* follow.

You shall love the Lord your God with all your heart, with all your soul and with all your mind.

You shall love your neighbour as yourself. → Mt 22:37,39

Photo credits

Martin Buhl p. 70, 79; Sylvia Buhl p. 12, 34, 57, 63, 67, 77, 80, 84; Peter Christoph Düren p. 14-15; Kilian Hasselmann p. 61; Alexander von Lengerke p. 72; Luc Serafin p. 8, 20, 26; Andreas Süß (*www.nightfever.org*) p. 6 © youmagazin p. 42-43